NOTE TO P/

Apologetics Press is a non-profit organization dedicated to the defense of New Testament Christianity. For over 30 years, we have provided faith-building materials for adults. We also have produced numerous products (*Discovery* magazine, our *Explorer Series*, children's tracts, and various books) for young people from infancy through high school. We now are pleased to present a new series of books.

The Apologetics Press Advanced Reader Series is a step up from our Early Reader Series. The Advanced Reader Series is aimed at children in 2nd-3rd grades. Although our Advanced Readers have about the same number of pages as our Early Readers, the Advanced Readers have more than twice as much text, as well as more advanced words.

With beautiful, full-color pictures and interesting facts about God's wonderfully designed Creation, your children will develop a greater love for reading and for their grand Designer.

We hope you enjoy using the Apologetics Press Advanced Reader Series to encourage your children to read, while at the same time helping them learn about God and His Creation.

Amazing Tails, Designed by God

by Eric Lyons

© 2009 Apologetics Press, Inc.

ISBN-13: 978-1-60063-014-9

Library of Congress: 2009905910

Layout and design: Rob Baker
Printed in China

APOLOGETICS PRESS, INC.
230 LANDMARK DRIVE
MONTGOMERY, AL 36117-2752

Amazing Tails

Tails

Designed by God

by Eric Lyons

God designed many animals with amazing tails. There are long tails and short tails, skinny tails and fat tails. Animals may use their tails to show happiness or

sadness. They may also use their tails to show when they are upset or afraid. God designed tails that can do and show many wonderful things.

Dogs often wag their tails quickly, back and forth, when they are happy and friendly. Dogs may stiffen their tails when they are angry. When a dog is afraid, it often puts its tail between its legs or lets it hang down low to the ground.

One of the most famous tails belongs to the beaver. God made the beaver's tail long and flat. As a beaver swims, it uses its tail like a boat's rudder, to steer where it needs to go. It also uses its tail for balance when standing on its hind legs.

When a beaver senses danger, it can make a loud noise by slapping its tail on the water. This alerts other beavers to get away and hide.

Birds may not be the first animals that come to mind when you think of tails, but God designed birds with some of the most beautiful tails in the animal kingdom. Peacocks have some of the biggest and most colorful tail feathers of any bird. They can grow to be more than four feet long.

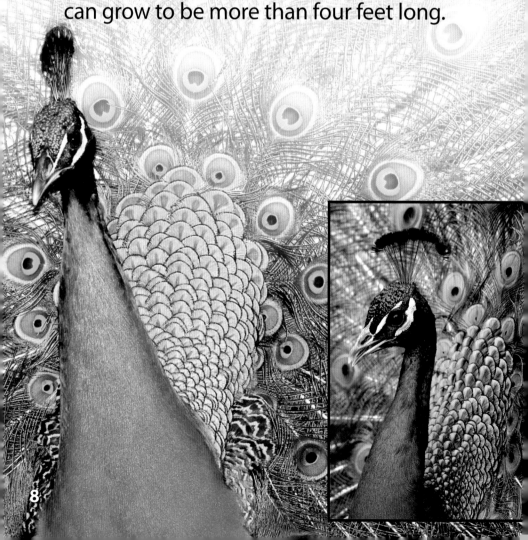

Birds use their feathered tails to do all sorts of things. When perched, a bird uses its tail feathers for balance. Birds can also use their tails to communicate with other birds.

The stiff tail feathers of woodpeckers support them perfectly as they peck on a tree in search of insects.

Like a rudder on the tail of an airplane, a bird's tail can help steer it while in flight. Its tail can also help produce lift while in the air. A wagging or flipping tail may show happiness, while tail fanning may be a bird's way of showing its strength or anger. A hawk spreads its tail feathers to soar, and folds them together when swooping down like a dart, to attack its prey.

Oklahoma's state bird, the scissor-tail fly-catcher, opens its tail feathers during flight so that they appear like scissors. These feathers are often longer than its body.

God did not have to "try out" tails on birds to see if they would be helpful. He knew they would be helpful all along. In His amazing wisdom, He created our flying, feathered friends on day five of Creation (Genesis 1:20-23), with many different, well-designed tails.

God gave the opossum a long, hairless prehensile (prē-HĔN-sǔl) tail. A prehensile tail is one that can wrap around and hold things. Opossums use their tails to hang from tree limbs for short periods of time. They also use their tails to carry grass and leaves to build their nests in trees.

Opossums are not the only animals with prehensile tails. Some monkeys have them as well. These monkeys use their tails like another hand, to hold food and tree branches, and to swing from one tree to another.

One way to tell monkeys from chimps is that most monkeys have tails, and chimps do not.

God designed rattlesnakes with "rattles" at the end of their tails. Rattlesnakes use their rattles to sound a warning when they are in danger.

The rattle of a rattlesnake is made up of hardened skin. Every time a rattlesnake sheds its skin, the rattle gets bigger.

God designed kangaroos with long, thick tails. When a kangaroo is not hopping, it moves slowly by balancing on its tail and front paws, and moving its feet forward. This is called "crawl-walking." Without tails, kangaroos would have a hard time crawl-walking.

The tail of a seahorse is very well designed. As with the opossum and certain monkeys, God gave the seahorse a prehensile (prē-HĔN-sŭl) tail. Do you remember what prehensile means?

Seahorses use their tails to wrap around seaweed and anchor themselves. This keeps fast water currents from carrying seahorses far away from their home.

A stingray's tail is not something with which you want to play. It is armed with very sharp, barbed spines. If a stingray is disturbed, it can whip its tail and drive its spines into the enemy. The stingray then releases poison, which causes painful stinging. The stingray is well named.

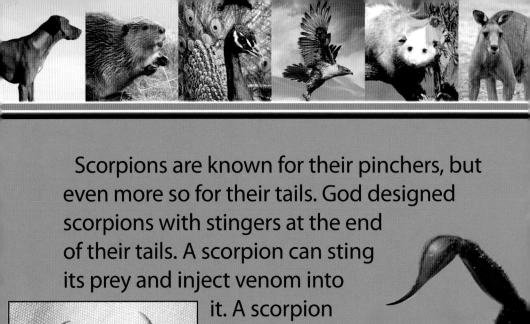

Scorpions are known for their pinchers, but even more so for their tails. God designed scorpions with stingers at the end of their tails. A scorpion can sting its prey and inject venom into it. A scorpion can also control how much venom it releases. A scorpion's stinger is a great defense device designed by God.

God designed a lizard called the Gila (HĒ-lŭ) monster with a bulky tail. As with a camel that can store fat in its hump, the Gila monster is able to store fat in its tail. It can go a long time without food by using the fat in its tail to survive.

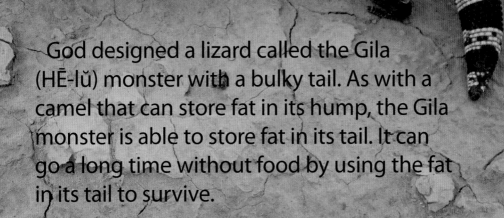

God designed the lobster's tail to keep the animal steady in rough waters. Its tail can also contract quickly so that the lobster can scoot away from danger.

Lobsters have perhaps the most famous tails in the world. Why are they so popular? Because they taste so good. People all over the world love to eat lobster "tail" meat dipped in butter. It is a favorite food of many Americans.

Foxes have long, bushy tails. When a fox is cold, it can curl up and wrap its tail over its nose and feet to stay warm. A fox's tail also helps the animal change directions quickly when hunting its prey or fleeing from danger.

The Bible tells a story about a man named Samson who caught 300 foxes. He put them in pairs by tying their tails together. Samson used the foxes to destroy his enemies' crops (Judges 15:4-5).

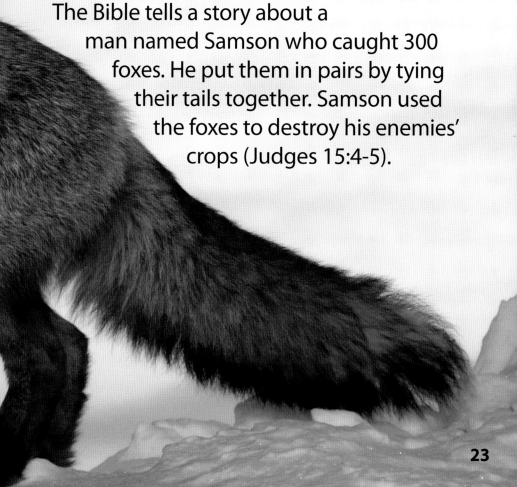

God gave many lizards the ability to lose their tails and grow new ones. This comes in very handy if an attacker grabs or bites the tail of a lizard. The lizard can dash away as soon as its tail breaks off. Over the next few months (or maybe years), many lizards can grow new tails.

The tail of a whale is called a fluke. A whale moves its fluke up and down in the water in order to propel itself forward. Just before they dive, whales raise their flukes up out of the water. The fluke of a blue whale can be as wide as 25 feet.

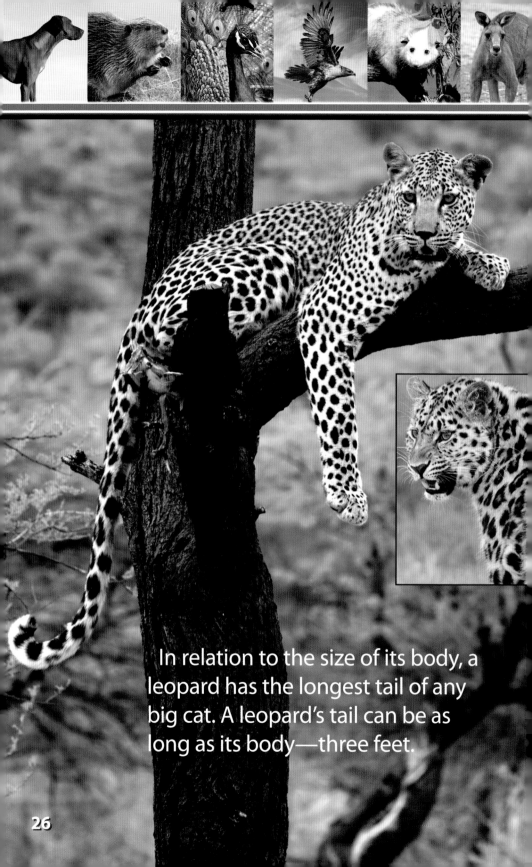

In relation to the size of its body, a leopard has the longest tail of any big cat. A leopard's tail can be as long as its body—three feet.

Even though the giraffe is known more for its long neck, it also has a very long tail. In fact, it has the longest tail of any land animal living today. It can grow to be eight feet long. A giraffe's tail keeps flies and other insects away.

The giraffe's tail is small compared to the tail of certain dinosaurs that once lived. The tail of *Diplodocus* was more than 40 feet long, which was more than twice the length of its body.

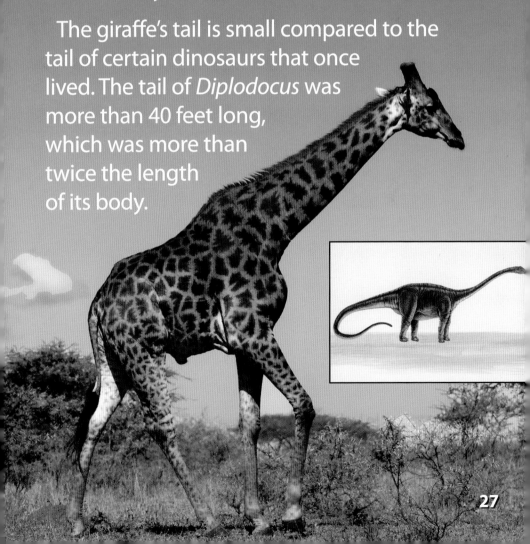

God once spoke to Job about an animal that ranked "first among the works of God," whose tail was so massive it swayed "like a cedar" (Job 40:17,19). What kind of animal was it? It is called "behemoth." But what exactly was this behemoth?

What animal's tail could best be described as "moving" or "swaying" **like a cedar**?

What animal grew a tail more than 40 feet long, that weighed thousands of pounds? Behemoth sounds more like one of the big plant-eating dinosaurs of the past than any animal alive today.

Illustration by Lewis Lavoie

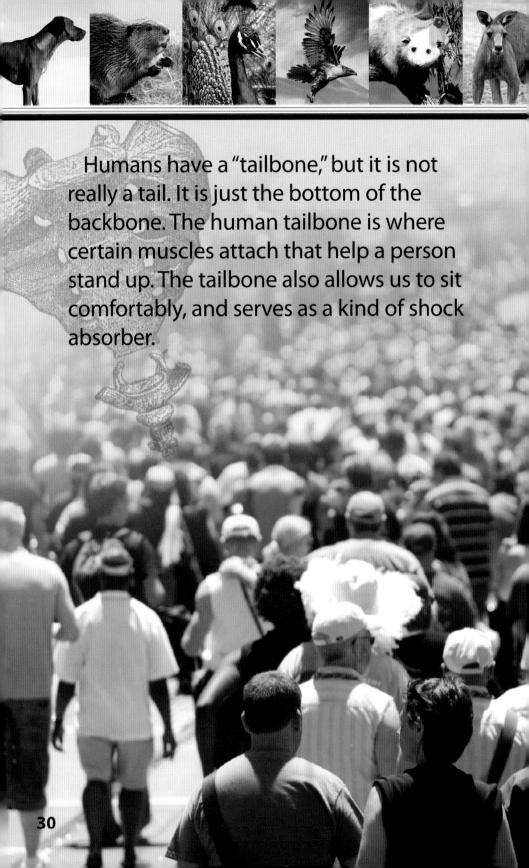

Humans have a "tailbone," but it is not really a tail. It is just the bottom of the backbone. The human tailbone is where certain muscles attach that help a person stand up. The tailbone also allows us to sit comfortably, and serves as a kind of shock absorber.

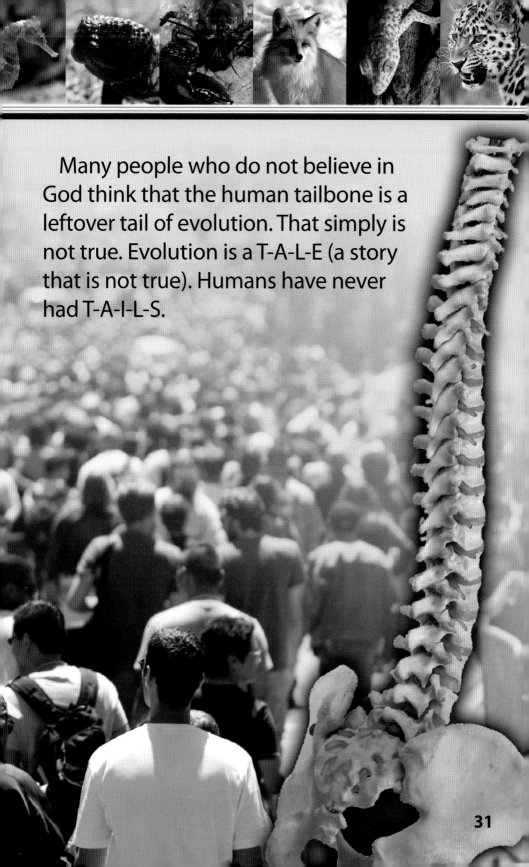

Many people who do not believe in God think that the human tailbone is a leftover tail of evolution. That simply is not true. Evolution is a T-A-L-E (a story that is not true). Humans have never had T-A-I-L-S.

God designed many different types of animals with amazing tails. Animals use tails to hang onto things. They use them to show what they are feeling. They use them to defend themselves against predators. Tails can also help animals keep their balance, or store fat that can help them when they do not have food to eat.

The theory of evolution may tell tales, but it cannot tell how all of these amazing animals got such well-designed tails. Tails are not accidents of evolution. They are amazing creations of God.